BRITISH HISTORY MAKERS

Julius Caesar

Claire Throp

raintree

Raintree is an imprint of Capstone Global Library Limited, a company incorporated in England and Wales having its registered office at 264 Banbury Road, Oxford, OX2 7DY – Registered company number: 6695582

www.raintree.co.uk
myorders@raintree.co.uk

Text © Capstone Global Library Limited 2017
The moral rights of the proprietor have been asserted.

Edited by Linda Staniford
Designed by Steve Mead
Picture research by Ruth Smith
Production by Tori Abraham
Originated by Capstone Global Library

ISBN 978 1 474 73409 7 (hardback)
20 19 18 17 16
10 9 8 7 6 5 4 3 2 1

ISBN 978 1 474 73414 1 (paperback)
21 20 19 18 17
10 9 8 7 6 5 4 3 2 1

British Library Cataloguing in Publication Data
A full catalogue record for this book is available from the British Library.

Acknowledgements
We would like to thank the following for permission to reproduce photographs:
Alamy: Classic Image, 26, INTERFOTO, 5, Lanmas, 11, Photo Researchers, Inc, 18; Capstone Press: cover, 6; Deposit Photos: kyolshin, 23; Dreamstime: Iurii Kuzo, 9; Getty Images: Culture Club, 16, Kean Collection, 22, Kean Collection/Hulton Archive, 17, Photo12/UIG, 24; Mary Evans Picture Library: cover; Newscom: akg-images, 21, Art Media Heritage Images, 14, The Print Collector Heritage Images, 15; Shutterstock: Aleks Melnik, cover, title page, Cris Foto, 13, Everett – Art, 25, Happy Art, cover, background design elements, HildaWeges Photography, 10, Jason Benz Bennee, 7, Joseph Sohm, 20, meunierd, 19, PLRANG ART, 12, pseudolongino, 4, Renata Sedmakova, 27, Toluk, cover, background design elements; Superstock: Fine Art Images, 8

We would like to thank Dr Mark Zumbuhl of the University of Oxford for his invaluable help in the preparation of this book.

Every effort has been made to contact copyright holders of material reproduced in this book. Any omissions will be rectified in subsequent printings if notice is given to the publisher.

All the Internet addresses (URLs) given in this book were valid at the time of going to press. However, due to the dynamic nature of the Internet, some addresses may have changed, or sites may have changed or ceased to exist since publication. While the author and publisher regret any inconvenience this may cause readers, no responsibility for any such changes can be accepted by either the author or the publisher.

Printed and bound in India

Some words are shown in bold, **like this**. You can find out what they mean by looking in the glossary.

Contents

Caesar's life 4

The Romans 6

Early life 8

The army 10

Political life 12

Gaul 14

Britain 16

War 20

Dictator and death 24

Legacy 26

Timeline 28

Glossary 30

Find out more 31

Index 32

Caesar's life

Julius Caesar is known as one of the greatest Roman **generals**. He was a **politician** who worked his way up to become **dictator**. In doing this, he put an end to the Roman **Republic**.

∽ FACT ∾

Caesar wrote about the wars he took part in, including his **invasions** of Britain. He did not always tell the truth, though!

The Romans

The Romans came from Rome in Italy. They **conquered** many countries. The main reason that the Romans were so successful was their army. The soldiers were well-trained and very disciplined.

The purple areas on this map show the countries that the Romans conquered.

BRITAIN

GERMANY

River Rhine

Carpathian Mountains

Atlantic Ocean

GAUL (France)

Alps

EUROPE

Pyrenees

River Danube

Black Sea

Caspian Sea

CORSICA

•Rome

Caucasus

SPAIN

SARDINIA

GREECE

SICILY

Mediterranean Sea

Euphrates River

Tigris River

0   500   1,000 Miles
0   500   1,000   1,500 Kilometres

•Jerusalem

MIDDLE EAST

EGYPT

AFRICA

Red

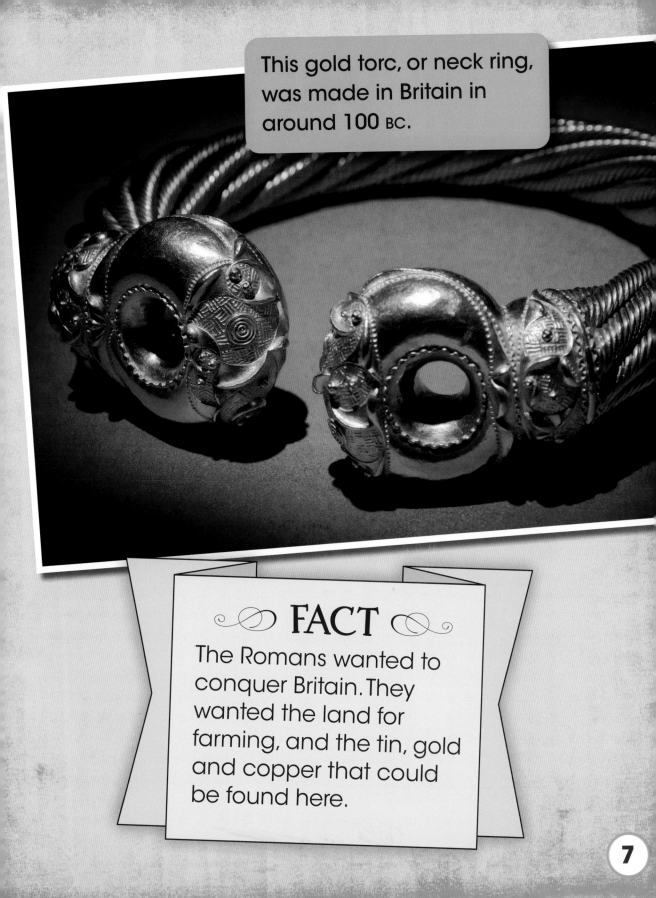

This gold torc, or neck ring, was made in Britain in around 100 BC.

⟬ FACT ⟭

The Romans wanted to conquer Britain. They wanted the land for farming, and the tin, gold and copper that could be found here.

Early life

Gaius Julius Caesar was born on 13 July 100 BC to Gaius Caesar and Aurelia. His family lived in Rome. As a child, he was good at sport. A famous public speaker, Marcus Antonius Gnipho, taught Caesar how to give brilliant speeches.

The army

Caesar joined the Roman army in 81 BC. During the Siege of Mytilene in 80 BC, Caesar bravely saved the life of another soldier. He was rewarded by being given the oak crown. This was the second highest award a soldier could be given. Caesar was a war hero.

✎ FACT ✎

Caesar was **kidnapped** by pirates in 75 BC. He told them they were not asking for enough money to let him go! Once free, he killed them all.

Political life

Caesar worked his way up the political ranks. He was helped by two men: Pompey and Crassus. In 61 BC, Caesar was made **governor** of the Roman **province** of Farther Spain. He then became **consul** of Rome in 59 BC. Consul was the highest political position that could be held in Rome.

Pompey

Crassus

❧ FACT ☙

Caesar, Pompey and Crassus became known as the First Triumvirate. A triumvirate means three people holding power.

Gaul

From 58 BC, Caesar was governor of Gaul (now France and Belgium). Many separate **tribes** lived there. Caesar began to defeat them one by one. Eventually, some of the tribes that were left united under one leader, Vercingetorix. But it was too late. In 52 BC, Caesar defeated Vercingetorix too.

Vercingetorix was captured by Caesar and surrendered to him.

FACT

Caesar was ruthless in Gaul. After one attack, he ordered that the hands of any survivors be cut off.

Britain

In August 55 BC, Caesar invaded Britain. As he sailed towards Dover, warriors were waiting along the top of the cliffs. Caesar was forced to land further along the coast and then fight for control of the beach. Many of Caesar's men were stranded in Gaul because of bad weather. After a few days of fighting, Caesar decided to leave Britain.

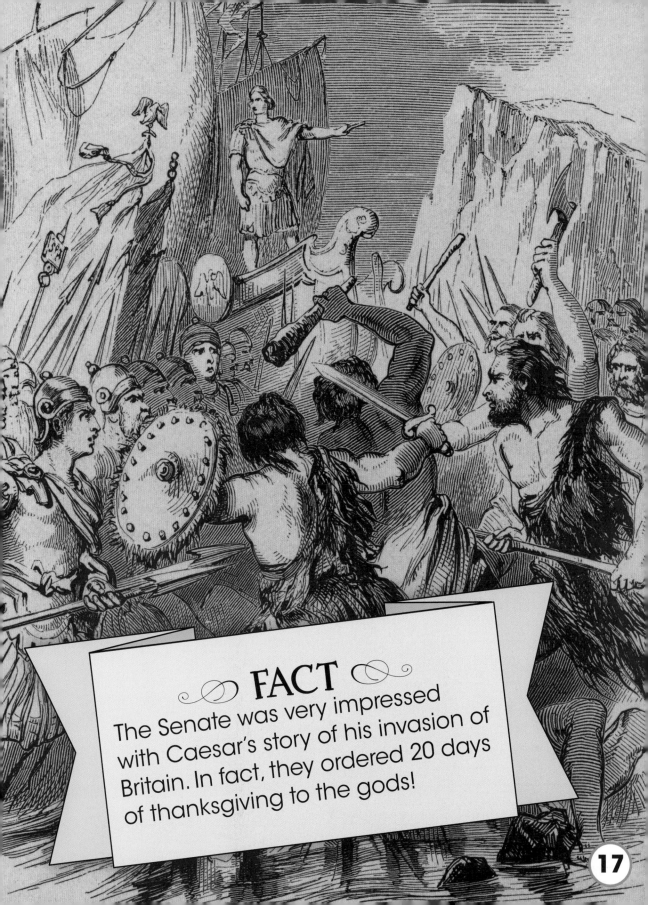

FACT

The Senate was very impressed with Caesar's story of his invasion of Britain. In fact, they ordered 20 days of thanksgiving to the gods!

In 54 BC, Caesar returned to Britain. His troops defeated some of the tribes and managed to get as far as the River Thames. King Cassivellaunus of the Catuvellauni tribe continually attacked the Romans. But even he eventually agreed to peace. Caesar couldn't complete his conquest of Britain, though. He had to return to Gaul to deal with a rebellion.

Caesar sailed up the River Thames with his troops.

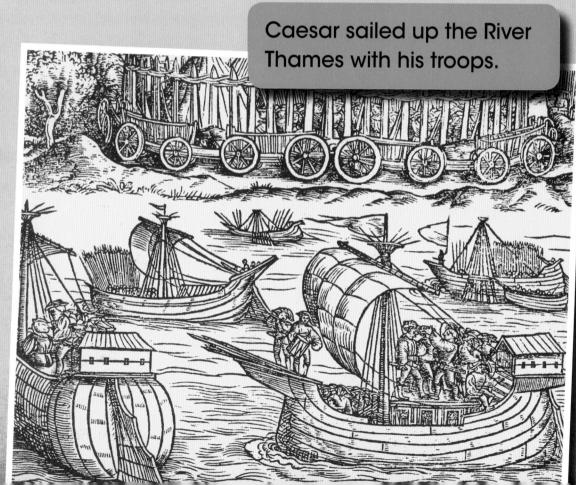

FACT

Caesar took 800 ships and at least 17,000 soldiers with him on his second invasion of Britain.

War

Some members of the **Senate**, including Pompey, were jealous of Caesar's popularity in Rome. They asked Caesar to hand over control of the army to the Senate or he would be seen as an enemy of Rome. He refused. In January 49 BC, Caesar crossed the Rubicon River into Italy with his army. This meant war.

Laws were made at the Senate house in Rome.

FACT

The Rubicon River formed part of Italy's border. It was against the law to cross the river with an army.

Pompey's job was to stop Caesar, but he was no match for him. Caesar defeated Pompey's forces in Spain in 49 BC. He then followed Pompey to Egypt. Pompey planned to ask Ptolemy, king of Egypt, for help, but Ptolemy killed Pompey.

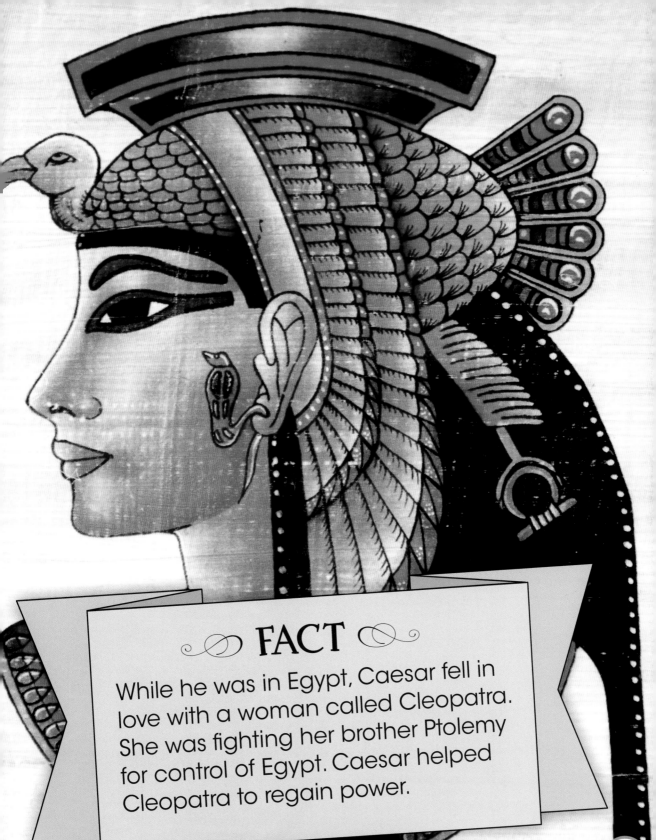

FACT

While he was in Egypt, Caesar fell in love with a woman called Cleopatra. She was fighting her brother Ptolemy for control of Egypt. Caesar helped Cleopatra to regain power.

Dictator and death

In 45 BC, Caesar became dictator of Rome. This meant a change in the style of government. Before, a number of people ruled together. Now just one man had power.

Caesar carried out many **reforms**. But not everyone was happy. When Caesar became dictator for life in 44 BC, a group of politicians murdered him.

A Roman coin showing Caesar as dictator

❧ FACT ❧

On 15 March, Caesar was stabbed 23 times on the steps of the Senate House in Rome.

Legacy

Caesar was one of the most successful Roman generals. He was a brave soldier and a clever politician. He conquered Gaul. His invasion of Britain led the way for later generals to triumph. Roman Emperor Claudius eventually conquered Britain in AD 43.

JULIUS CÆSAR.

～∾ FACT ∾～

Caesar was born in the month of Quintilis in the old Roman calendar. It was renamed July in his honour.

Timeline

BC

100 Gaius Julius Caesar born in July

81 Caesar joins the Roman army

61–60 Caesar is made governor of the Roman province of Farther Spain

59 Caesar is appointed a consul with help from Pompey and Crassus, and the three of them are known as the First Triumvirate

58 Caesar becomes governor of Gaul and conquers more land for Rome

55 First invasion of Britain

54 Second invasion of Britain

49 Senate asks Caesar to hand over control of the army to them, but he refuses; this leads to war

49 Caesar defeats Pompey in Spain and follows him to Egypt; Pompey is murdered

49 Caesar stays in Egypt over the winter and falls in love with Queen Cleopatra

45 Caesar returns to Rome as dictator, and carries out reforms

44 On 15 March, Caesar is murdered

AD

43 The army of Emperor Claudius conquers Britain

Glossary

conquer defeat and take control of an enemy

consul one of two generals who jointly ran the government in Rome

dictator someone who has complete control of a country, often ruling it unfairly

general highest rank in the army

governor person elected to be the head of government of a state

invasion when a country's military forces enter another country to take it over

kidnapped when a person is held against their will

politician someone who runs for a government office

province country outside Rome that was ruled by a Roman governor

reform change for the better in the way things are done, particularly in government

republic government where the people elect a small group of people to make decisions for everyone

Senate law-making body in ancient Rome

tribe group of people who share the same language and way of life

Find out more

Books

Gory Gladiators, Savage Centurions and Caesar's Sticky End: A Menacing History of the Unruly Romans (Awfully Ancient), Kay Benham (Wayland, 2016)

Julius Caesar, Anita Ganeri (Collins, 2015)

Julius Caesar and the Romans (History Starting Points), David Gill (Franklin Watts, 2016)

Websites

www.bbc.co.uk/guides/zqbnfg8
Read about what it was like to be in the Roman army.

www.dkfindout.com/uk/history/ancient-rome
Find out all you could ever want to know about ancient Rome.

Places to visit

British Museum
Great Russell Street, London WC1B 3DG
The British Museum has a room full of objects from Roman Britain.

National Roman Legion Museum
High St, Caerleon, Newport NP18 1AE
Visit this museum to see how Roman soldiers lived.

Index

Cassivellaunus, 18
Claudius, Emperor of Rome, 29
Claudius, Roman Emperor, 26
Cleopatra, 23, 29
Crassus, 12–13, 28

Egypt, 22–23, 29

Gaul, 14, 15, 16, 18, 28

invasion of Britain, 16, 18–19, 26, 28

Julius Caesar, 4, 26, 28–29
    as dictator of Rome, 24, 29
    birth, 8, 28
    childhood, 8
    death, 24–25, 29
    governor of Gaul, 14–15
    in politics, 12
    in the army, 10

Pompey, 12–13, 20, 22, 28–29
Ptolemy, 22–23

Romans, 6, 7
    army, 6, 10
Rubicon River, 20–21

Vercingetorix, 14